The Journey
from Lost to Found

The Journey
from Lost to Found

THE SEARCH THAT
BEGINS WITH THE END
OF A RELATIONSHIP

Susan Jeffers, Ph.D.

Fawcett Columbine · New York

A Fawcett Columbine Book
Published by Ballantine Books

Copyright © 1993 by Susan Jeffers, Ph.D.

All rights reserved under International and Pan-American
Copyright Conventions. Published in the United States by
Ballantine Books, a division of Random House, Inc., New
York, and simultaneously in Canada by Random House
of Canada Limited, Toronto.

Library of Congress Catalog Card Number: 93-91087

ISBN: 0-449-90925-5

Cover design by Georgia Morrissey
Cover photo © K. Muto/Photonica

Manufactured in the United States of America

First Ballantine Books Trade Paperback Edition:
August 1994

10 9 8 7 6 5 4 3 2 1

To the light within us all . . .

My life is beautiful,
I have it all . . .
But even in the sunshine,
One has to cry sometimes.

Contents

Preface

The contents of this book may surprise you. Long before I became an author of self-help books and a teacher in the area of personal growth, I was very fearful and needy of help myself. It was 1972. My first marriage was crumbling and I was feeling very empty and lost.

To help me get through this difficult, often overwhelming, period of my life, I would find solace in sometimes jotting down the feelings I was experiencing, usually on any piece of paper that happened to be handy at the time . . . an old envelope, a wrinkled sales slip, a gum wrapper, a notepad . . . or whatever. Later, when I would discover one of my scribblings at the bottom of my purse or lying somewhere around the house, I would throw it into a little box sitting on my shelf.

Two years passed. One Sunday afternoon when I had some time on my hands, I opened the little box and began to arrange my many pieces of paper in chronological order. I was astounded at the sequence of discovery that emerged. On these pieces of paper, collected over a two-year period, I was able to trace the Journey of a person who travelled from a place called Lost to a place called Found. My Journey included blame, despair, hurt, anger, discovery, laughter, joy, bliss, and every other human emotion. Little did I know that these thoughts, written over time, would be the seeds of much that I write about and teach today.

Whether you are in a relationship or not, you will see yourself in much of what you are going to read. Many of you have made the same Inner Journey as I have and will identify with my struggle and ultimate sense of triumph.

Many of you are still feeling lost. My experience will give you the faith that, step by step, it is possible for you to pull yourself out of your pain and loneliness . . . and find your way Home. Always remember that you are not alone. You are a part of the human family. And each of us, in our own way, has to make this poignant, profound . . . and sometimes painful . . . Journey from Lost to Found.

In the
Beginning

We thought one married and lived happily
ever after;
> *We didn't know* that relationships
> require hard work . . .

We thought we couldn't ask for what
we needed;
> *We didn't know* that no one is a mind
> reader . . .

We thought all of our needs should have been
filled with marriage;
> *We didn't know* what our most
> important need was—a sense of
> self . . .

We thought our becoming one made us whole;
    We didn't know two whole people
        were necessary from the start . . .

We thought he had to be strong and
    take care of her;
        We didn't know we were supposed to
            take care of each other . . .

We thought it was disloyal to grow as an
    individual;
        We didn't know how stifling too much
            togetherness could be . . .

We thought when the other grew, it was
    a threat;
        We didn't know we were each good
            enough and shouldn't feel
                threatened . . .

We thought those who asked for help
    were weak;
        We didn't know everyone needs
            help . . .

We thought money would make us secure;
    We didn't know that security meant
      knowing you can make it—
        with or without money . . .

We thought the other wasn't giving;
    We didn't know we weren't
      receiving . . .

He thought I was happy;
    He didn't know how frightened
      I was . . .

I thought he was happy;
    I didn't know how frightened
      he was . . .

We didn't know . . .
    We just didn't know . . .
      There was so much we didn't
      know . . .

The End
of an Era

So many of us live our lives with a feeling of depression born from our imagined helplessness. We depend on others to provide our happiness—seemingly unable to find it ourselves.

What is it that we *really* want?

Most of us don't even know . . . that we don't know . . . what we want out of life.

We don't know . . . that we don't know . . . what makes us happy.

All we know is that our mate isn't funny all
the time,
　　or clever all the time,
　　or considerate all the time,
　　or rich all the time,
　　or handsome all the time,
　　or whatever . . . all the time,
not recognizing that if he were all those things
all of the time, *we would still be looking for more.*

Such an impossible burden we place on people we *pretend* to love! Asking them to give us
what we want, when we don't even know
what we're looking for!

And so, the years pass. The resentment grows all around and we blame each other, instead of understanding, "Hey, I'm asking you the impossible! I'm asking you to give me myself!"

Slowly and imperceptibly, it becomes too late. The bitterness and hostility are too much to live with. And we wake up one morning and say, *"My God, what happened?"*

I don't turn you on any more,
  That's a real turn off;
You don't let me in any more,
  I prefer to stay out.

Your fear creates a need for separation; mine creates a need for closeness. Who said opposites attract?

I feel your love . . . and I feel your total resistance to loving me.

When I feel your hostility, I feel ugly. It is so difficult for me to reach out to you then. I withdraw and become hostile as well. It's such a pity. All that we are really both asking for is to be loved.

When I feel your hostility, YOU become ugly. If I could only have compassion for the wounded child behind your mask. But it's so hard to have compassion for someone you want to punch in the face!

You have in your head a picture about what our life is supposed to be. You expect that I will fit right into your picture. You forget that I, too, have a picture about what our life is supposed to be. And right now, you don't fit my picture!

I wonder why we always demand that it be the way "it's supposed to be." Why can't we simply enjoy the way it is?

Don't insist I behave in a certain way because society says I'm supposed to. Just look around! What does society know anyway!

It's time I start doing things because I choose to do them, not because I'm supposed to do them. It's time I start writing my own script!

As my daughter once beseeched me, "If you can't wear whatever socks you want, what's left in life?!?"

You started out as my best friend, but you have become my worst critic. I don't think that's what friendship is about!

Whoever he wanted all those years is not the me that is emerging. The more I become **ME** the less he likes me . . . and the more I like myself.

I have to be who *I* want me to be . . . whatever the price.

He never really loved **ME.** He *loved loving* me.
He loved the image of me that he created as
his wife . . . but he didn't really love **ME.**

No, he didn't really love **ME** . . . any more
than I really loved **HIM.**

A special friend once told me, "He sets you a banquet table and never brings you any food."

He seems empty to me . . . an empty suit. Is he empty? Or am I?

It appeared from the outside looking in that I had it all, yet I was starving. We both were. It's hard to give to someone when you are empty inside.

Before I could change, I had to recognize that life is too short to walk around feeling . . .

> *angry* all the time,
> *hurt* all the time,
> *empty* all the time,
> *alone* all the time.

The beginning was glorious because we were playing fairy-tale roles. We wanted it to last forever.

Alas! Things don't last forever. They must change and grow. Or, they will stagnate and die.

He was the King in the castle. He must have
felt terribly threatened when I wanted to share
the throne. Once you've ruled the Kingdom,
it's hard to let it go.

Some couples grow together. We only grew apart . . . so far apart that our arms couldn't reach each other any more.

How difficult it is to accept the end of an era. But, perhaps what is more difficult is to *recognize* the end of an era.

I tried so hard to hide from myself the possibility of separation. That was just too unacceptable for my mind to accept.

I finally perceived that in order for me to become the person I wanted to be, I had to end my fairy-tale marriage. It would be, as I learned, like dying and returning from the dead.

I remember the despair . . . the insecurity of feeling I couldn't survive on my own. Was there anyone else out there for me? Or was he the only drink of water in the desert?

We can't split up . . .
>　　How could I tell my mother!
We can't split up . . .
　　It would hurt the children!
We can't split up . . .
　　I couldn't survive alone!
We can't split up . . .
　　There's not enough money!
We can't split up . . .
　　I would never find anyone else!
We can't split up . . .
　　It would mean I've failed!
We can't split up . . .
　　He's such a good catch!

We must split up . . .
　　Or I will die . . . .

It's reassuring how the spirit of survival in all of us makes us subtly prepare for the ending of a relationship.

We look around, we fantasize, we develop a skill, a hobby, new friends. We read books dealing with the subjects of self-esteem, divorce, "making it," managing money. We become aware of other couples who are divorcing. We find ourselves seeking out models . . . those who've made it to the other shore.

Slowly, but surely, we prepare for the inevitable—the end of an era.

Sometimes doors are closed for us, giving us no choice but to move forward. It's nice to think our most difficult times are blessings in disguise!

While some endings may be difficult to accept, acceptance blessedly ends all the confusion—confusion that results from trying to fit old patterns and responses into healthier ones that are just emerging. We learn we just can't put the two together any more . . . no matter how much our fear makes us try.

Without accepting the end of one era, we can't throw the full strength of our being into another. We ultimately discover that there's nothing as powerful as a made-up-mind!

The nature of growth is that it is always pulling us forward . . . despite how much we try to drag our feet!

Looking back, we clung so close—so desper-
ately close—for so many years . . .

I wonder what we were looking for . . .

Ourselves, I guess.

The
Search

I didn't know it was going to hurt so much. I wanted the marriage to end, yet I wasn't prepared for all the pain . . . the emptiness in the pit of my stomach . . . tearing me apart. Is there anything left to look forward to? Nothing matters. I feel so alone.

Sometimes the darkness overcomes me.
Bewilderment. Panic. Exhaustion. Nausea.
Hunger. It has to get better!

The unrelenting anger wells up inside and paralyzes me. "How could you" . . . I say to all those significant ones who have caused me pain . . . especially him. I sit there staring into space, my heart pounding. Then the tears come. So much hurt!

When and how will I get rid of all that pain?
I don't know. In the meantime, I'll just have
to let it be.

Life was incomplete with you . . . Now it is incomplete without you . . .

I feel like someone has thrown me in the water to teach me how to swim. Maybe later I'll be thankful for the opportunity. Now, I simply feel like I'm drowning.

I'm lost! A whole Saturday to do anything I want! I've searched my mind a hundred times and I can't think of anything I want to do! Once again the terror comes. There is nothing I can do to stop it. Everyone is out there with someone. I know it. I am the only one who is alone.

Will I always feel I'm on the outside looking in? Like a poor little girl peering longingly through the window on a cold snowy night, yearning to be part of the happy family sitting cozily before the fire?

For the first time in so many years, I am without a MAN. I realize now how much of an appendage I was all those years. There was no me without HIM.

Time with my children, my girlfriends, my colleagues—it was all filling time until I could be with HIM. Without HIM, everything was second best. My world did not count. I lived in his. Without HIM I was just drifting, hoping to find someone else's world to belong to.

I hope, I hope, I hope I can stop searching soon.

I hope, I hope, I hope another HE will soon appear so I can go on with my life.

I never realized how little I did over the years that was really me. I had no real friends, no hobbies, no interests that weren't totally part of being a couple. Is it any wonder I feel lost?

Where do I hide from myself . . . that I need someone constantly to sustain me? My first response to learning that I will be alone for an evening or a Saturday is ABANDONMENT. The only one who really abandons me ever, is me! It seems I have been gone so long.

It is strange how difficult it is to find out something as basic as "Who Am I." "Listen to the cues," I'm told. But the cues are so faint. The voice inside me has been walled off with so many layers of conditioning. Will I ever be able to hear that little voice inside me that is trying to be heard? I can't believe I have travelled so far away from the core of my very being.

The Journey inward begins. I start to ask myself such questions as, "What FEELS good?" It's funny but I never paid much attention to that before. Somehow my life had been all taken care of. I never knew how high a price one pays for being taken care of . . .

So many "firsts" without HIM . . .

Attending	my first party	without HIM
Living through	my first holiday season	without HIM
Furnishing	my first apartment	without HIM
Taking	my first trip	without HIM
Developing	my first hobby	without HIM
Hosting	my first dinner party	without HIM

Each step taken is a step into the unknown. I feel like a child learning to walk. But with each step I feel a little surer of my ability to handle my life.

But when will the fear go away?

Slowly, very slowly, yet with giant steps forward, time begins to have meaning.

And suddenly one day *IT* appears. A connection. An exquisite moment. A moment when everything seems OK, safe, perfect. A moment that I'd created for myself. I hang on to it for dear life—but, sadly, it vanishes. What is left, however, is the knowledge that *IT* can exist.

I asked myself what it was that I had con-
nected with. And then suddenly, I knew—**I
HAD CONNECTED WITH MYSELF!!!**
For the first time in my life, **I FELT
WHOLE!**

Those delicious moments of wholeness were to come and go—appearing more and more often and staying around for longer periods of time. And very slowly, but very surely, I stopped defining myself in terms of a relationship. The voice inside became clearer and clearer every day, letting me know . . . I was coming Home.

Moments
Along the Way

My heart is pounding right now, clueing me into the fact that I'm scared. I ask myself, "scared of what?"

I saw someone die today.

Am I scared about the fragility of life? I don't think so.

Am I scared about being alone? No, that's not it.

Am I scared about not doing all the things in life that I want to do? **YES! That's it!**

I have so much I want to do. I want to . . . I can't . . . my job . . . my responsibilities. But what about me? When? When do I sit on that beach and just write? When? When do I see the sights I want to see? When? When won't I be afraid to take risks?

I'm afraid if I soon don't start doing what I want to do for me, I'll never be ready to die. After all, what is death? The end of life. But what if you've hardly lived?

I want to let go of so many things that are familiar and bring me security—and I'm scared. I gave up a relationship which didn't work and in many ways I'm still not free. My fear keeps me a prisoner.

Risks! Risks! I must learn to take risks! It's the difference between being dead and alive.

Wouldn't it be wonderful to face new experiences with delicious anticipation instead of feeling that my teeth are being pulled!

Why is change—any kind of change—so frightening?

If you change things often, does the fear go away?

We shout "FREEDOM" and don't know what it means. It is a borrowed word. When we finally have a chance to taste it, all we can shout is "HELP!"

I thought life was supposed to be comfortable. This thought kept me from experiencing and growing. I've recently learned that *LIFE IS NOT COMFORTABLE!* It is . . .

Alive!
Rich!
Scary!
Challenging!
Dynamic!
Changing!
Painful!
Joyful!

But seldom comfortable . . . if you are growing! DEAD is comfortable—about as comfortable as you can get.

I wonder if I can learn to be comfortable being uncomfortable!?!

Sometimes I feel that I am only glancing at things I should embrace.

I have to remind myself to keep pushing past my fatigue. That's the only way to get where one wants to go. Climbing back into bed with the covers over my head may feel good for the moment. But life is beckoning me to come out and play.

Part of me wants to surrender—to give up trying to "become." I want someone to become for me.

It isn't easy, life. Sometimes even going toward the fun times seems too much of an effort. I guess "easy" is for children! It's time for me to grow up.

I found out recently that I am very shy. It's strange, I never thought of myself that way. In my little world, I feel quite secure. But take me out of my world and I'm afraid to reach out, to participate.

I never realized it before. I had a marvelous defense . . . I made everyone "out there" boring. A perfect excuse to withdraw. What I was really feeling was "I don't belong. I'm uncomfortable here. I'm afraid they won't like me." I guess it was *ME* that I really thought was boring!

It's an impossible situation, I guess. I meet few men who like strong women and I refuse to be weak. So what does all that mean? It means I don't have a man . . . and some man out there doesn't have me. What a pity!

You can have anything in life, but you can't have everything! We have to make choices . . . and then love our choices. I guess that's the real meaning of "having it all"!

I've made a choice . . . a man who loves who I am. Or no man. I must learn that sometimes loneliness goes with the latter. And that's OK.

One choice that I've made is that I'll never allow myself to be dominated again. I must learn to take responsibility for my life and not blame any HIM.

How do I handle my fear of a man dominating me? I dominate him.

How do I do this?

> I flirt with other men . . .
> I get angry and sarcastic . . .
> I talk about him in the most negative
>   terms . . .
> I invalidate him . . .
> I judge him . . .
> I don't let him in . . .
> I leave . . .

What makes us so afraid to reach out and say, "Love me." It's so much easier to say, "Get out of my life. I don't need anyone!" And then we wonder why we are lonely.

It's always relationships that touch the land of tears that lies deep within me. When there is no relationship, I can live with the dull throb of insecurity interjected with some magical moments here and there.

When I am in a relationship, my insecurity hits me squarely in the face. Perhaps that's why relationships are so valuable. They lead the way to the needy child within . . . the child we have neglected to love. We would be wise to give it the kindness and caring it deserves.

I feel icy cold sometimes, feeling I give myself away. I guess that's a sign of death to the Soul.

I know I don't love me. I don't know how to love me. Maybe just knowing is a good first step.

I don't know how to relate to a man. I'm so afraid he'll put me down. So I act superior all the time. I'm the know-it-all. Does everyone know how much I have to learn?

Sometimes I feel so inferior, it's disgusting.
Sometimes I feel so superior, it's disgusting.

How many times do I have to repeat the same pattern? I want to tell him what I am really feeling. I don't have any reason to withhold. The problem is that I mask what I am really feeling even to myself. Therefore, I can't tell him the truth. I don't know the truth about myself until it's too late—and then I hurt.

Our society is so "advanced," yet too many of us are unable to fill even the most basic of human needs—the need to communicate and to touch.

age of transition makes a very strange breed:

"I want to be free!"	"Why aren't you there when I need you?"
"Don't tell me what to do!"	"Why aren't you taking care of me?"
"I believe in equality!"	"What do you mean you want me to pay half the rent?"

That's me talking! It's amazing how much I remind myself of some 15-year-olds I know!

I have made the decision that I will live my life with dignity and love and caring and that I am going to push through all the barriers that keep me from doing so. Yes, that's my decision. We all have that choice.

To how many people do I need to say . . . "I'm sorry. I didn't support you when you needed me. I needed to support myself instead. I'm still not as strong as I'd like to be. It makes me very sad. I know I'm getting there, but I'm sorry if I hurt you along the way"?

That many, huh?

To the men in my life . . . How do I want to relate to you?

I want . . .

> *to make you only one part of my life . . . not my whole life,*

> *to give you the space to be where you are . . . not where I want you to be,*

> *to stop being defensive . . . and really hear what you are saying,*

> *to relate as a peer . . . not to make myself either superior or inferior,*

> *to reach out when you criticize . . . not withdraw or become hostile,*

to express my feelings—now—with no game playing,

to more easily recognize my "tapes" and relate to you as you . . . not someone who hurt me in the past,

to be clear about what I want from you . . . so I can tell you,

to love the wounded child within you unconditionally . . . and not hurt it any more than it's already been hurt.

An insight: When I give, I expect something back. If I expect to get something back, then I am not giving . . . I am only exchanging. I must ask myself,

"Do I really know how to give?"

I always thought of myself as a giving person. I wonder how many other lies I've told myself.

I realize I'm a person who can't take. If someone is there for me emotionally, I don't handle it very well. I can't reach out when I am
in pain. Maybe I'm frightened of being weak
after working so hard to become strong. If I let
someone in, will I lose myself again? I'm afraid
to take that chance.

My head still thinks of exquisite moments only with a man, yet my most sublime moments have been without a man—moments I've created for myself. When will I stop listening to my mind and start paying attention to my heart?

More alone-time is necessary. Why do I shy
away from being alone? Habit, I guess. In the
past I was so accustomed to feeling abandoned
when I was alone. It's still surprising to know
that some of my most pleasurable times are my
alone-times.

No longer am I standing there waiting for some man to catch up to me. Rather, I am standing there waiting for **ME** to catch up to me!

I know I am growing. I am alone. There is no one there for me right now. I saw two people kissing today. Instead of feeling the old loneliness I used to feel, I only felt their joy.

Joyful feelings are so new to me. I spent so much of my life feeling sad or angry or down or rotten or cheated. In truth, I had it all, all along. I just never saw it before. And I lose sight of it too often now. Talk about needing glasses!

On my bus ride home tonight, I learned two
things about me . . .

> Even if I'm alone, there are a lot of
> people in my life who love me . . . and
> I love bus rides!

It's very complicated! I recently learned that all failure is, is getting what you don't want. Success is getting what you want. Pictures create the failure—expectations gone awry.

If you support whatever happens—you can't fail. Supporting it means acknowledging that that's the way it is . . . and it's OK with you. What is, is.

When you don't support the way it is, you fail. After all, what is failure? A picture not filled.

Whew! It makes so much sense! Why is it so difficult to understand?

It's amusing that things never turn out the way we plan. When am I going to learn that the picture I create in my head has absolutely no influence on if and when it comes? When am I going to stop trying to control the future . . . and simply let things happen? Wouldn't that be a relief!

I have to learn how to let go. What I try to control ends up controlling me. I tell myself, "Let go. Let go. Let go." Sometimes it's hard.

Sometimes I feel I could conquer the world.
Sometimes I feel so tired. I fantasize at those
"tired" times that I will just sit down in the
middle of the street and someone will come
and pick me up and take care of me. I don't
feel that so much any more, though. The
world seems more and more manageable as I
feel better and better about myself.

A beautiful woman taught me, "Say YES to your Universe. Whatever happens, say yes to your Universe." Those words meant little until I allowed their meaning to penetrate my experience. "Whatever happens, happens. Go with it and learn." When I am willing to go with my experiences—good or bad—instead of fighting them, it is such a relief! My life just seems to flow!

For a few days now, I have been really wanting to take care of myself. I feel an openness to letting things in. It's a new feeling . . . the realization that I can do whatever I want to do . . . experience whatever I want to experience.

A trip just opened up for me. Great! I want to go! Done!! I don't have to get "permission" from anyone. I won't pine for anyone when I'm away. I won't feel guilty.

I know there are advantages to a relationship, but I'm beginning to realize that there are also incredible advantages to being unattached! That is . . . once you've connected with yourself.

It was not long ago that I felt controlled. I felt my freedom was being taken away.

First came the *revelation*: **I allowed my freedom to be taken away!**

Then came the *revolution*: **"NO! I won't do what you demand of me."**

The thrill of entitlement! The freedom of entitlement! Whatever the cost!

And how does it feel to be free . . .

    to wear the clothes I've always wanted
      to wear . . .

    to say the things I've always wanted to
      say . . .

    to dance the way I've always wanted
      to dance . . .

    to do what I've always wanted to
      do . . .

    to be what I've always wanted to
      be . . .

Well, I'll tell you . . .

Whenever I feel that freedom, I become ex-
hilarated!!! I have unbounded energy. I could

dance all night and all day. My creativity is unleashed. I want to cry at the pleasure I find within myself.

Very often when I feel free, I feel afraid—but less and less as time goes by. And I know for the first time in my life . . .

I have a chance!

The lesson of being free is so simple that it eludes us. We think of freedom as the unencumbered life, but it is really the unencumbered self. To be free is simply to act on one's truth . . . and to allow no one else to obscure that truth.

I can't blame him. The lack of freedom I felt was of my own creation. In my effort to gain approval from him, I was denying myself. It was my choice. I realize I cannot blame him . . . or anyone else . . . for my choices in life.

I giggled as I walked down the street the other day as I realized there is nothing anyone can threaten to take away from me. I am alone now and I am whole.

When I stop demanding of myself and simply ask "what do I want?," I have made great strides toward self-fulfillment.

As I live each day getting more and more out of life . . . in terms of what I want out of life . . . my old fear of death and aging diminishes greatly.

The search to reveal the hidden layers of me goes on and on. I used to ask myself when will it end! I now realize it never ends.

We keep unpeeling the layers until the day we die. It's a relief to know I'm not a failure because I haven't hit the core. Yet I wonder when I die, what part of me I will never have known . . .

I used to look to other worlds thinking "I wonder what it's like over there." I always seemed to be searching for something. I realize I'm no longer searching. It's all here. It's all about seeing the richness in each new experience. Good or bad, it's nice to have tasted it.

The Journey:
    From confusion. . .
        to anger. . .
        to hurt. . .
        to pain. . .
        to power. . .
        to love. . .

Wouldn't it be wonderful if we could skip a few steps along the way?!?

There is such bittersweet pain in the joy that comes from finally beginning to understand the secret of life . . . and I am finally beginning to understand.

And what is the big secret to life . . . the secret I've been avoiding? **I AM TOTALLY RE-SPONSIBLE FOR MY HAPPINESS!** It's so frightening . . . yet filled with opportunity! No one to blame, no one to make wrong and ultimately no one to turn to . . . except myself.

Coming
Home

How did it happen? How did the feeling of contentment that eluded me for so long come to be? I don't know. I just "lived into it" somehow.

I was constantly told "Find yourself! Find yourself!" How do you find yourself? It's funny. I finally found myself and I don't know how I did it. I don't even know what was "found!" All I know is that I now feel content. I feel good with me.

I love other people and I need them. But I also need whole weekends of being totally alone—an impossibility just months ago. And when I need company, it doesn't have to be a HIM.

It can be my female friends, my children, my mother . . .

I'm no longer on the outside looking in. I'm at the center of my own Universe. It's such a warm and wonderful world that way. I'm never excluded. It's always *my* party.

I feel so good! I don't know why exactly. Nothing in my life is resolved—no permanence—which such a few years ago was my imagined harbor of safety.

In a few days that one permanent fantasy—my marriage—will be over—legally. But the peace in that! I have done so much for myself. Perhaps that's the joy I feel.

I recall the feelings of helplessness, hopelessness, just like it was yesterday—yet it really was a lifetime ago.

To find one's own energy—own purpose—
takes time. At first it is very dark. The loneliness is frightening. However, once we push
through it, we find a tremendous reservoir of
power. Without knowing this power is within
us, how can we love anyone else? Fear is a
great barrier to love!

At first, it is difficult to break old habits—it takes time. I guess the toughest habit to break is dependence. We expect someone to carry our burden and we call it love.

There is so much to learn about who I am. Each day brings new opportunities and new insights. Each entry in my book of life, each new experience—whether good or bad—I now see as an opportunity to "play," an opportunity to be aware of how I handle my feelings. I have learned not to judge myself, just to recognize and be aware. I know this acceptance of who I am will allow what I can become.

The bittersweet memories of it all. A wise man told me a long time ago . . .

"We are all travellers. Nothing is permanent. We are like fruit trees. The beautiful petals blow away and sweet fruit emerges. We cannot mourn the fact that the petals have blown away. We must rejoice at the sweet fruit we have become. We must understand that had the petals not blown away, we would not be what we are today. There is unhealthiness in attaching ourselves to things in a world where change is growth. We learn through the scars and hurt, what is right and wrong for us. We must act as a filter, letting in the good and discarding the bad. We can't live with the anger and the hurt. We have to let go—forgive and forget. Remember that you are who you are today because of those past experiences.

Let it go. Let it all go. When you can let go, you are left with tranquility.''

When I finally let go, I understood for the first time what he was talking about.

I feel like I'm getting younger. Everything I am learning is making me feel lighter, more childlike. I have stopped taking myself so seriously—even in my intensely serious moments. I guess part of me loves the drama of those gallantly played scenes. I find myself applauding constantly—and laughing hysterically.

What a beautiful Sunday . . . ME alone with ME. I never knew how content I could be.

It is morning. Arising late. A hot cup of coffee (there's nothing like that first cup of coffee). The Sunday *Times*. The music of my apartment or the quiet of my apartment . . . *as I choose*. I write, I dance. Even doing my laundry seems special today. Even paying my bills is a reminder that I can take care of myself and live my life . . . *as I choose*.

It is late afternoon. Some peanuts and a cup of tea as I watch the lightning's magnificence and hear the mighty claps of thunder. I delve into my book and a cozy nap overtakes me.

A beautiful night is yet to come. It's a pity that tomorrow it has to end. The way I feel right now I could stay alone with ME forever.

My life is so rich right now. I know why. Everything I do, I choose to do. I'm no longer filling time. It took me so long to be able to choose anything. I remember those early days of being alone. I couldn't fill an hour. Now, not only can I fill an hour, I can fill a lifetime.

I tried a singles party tonight. I figured, "What the heck! I'm always complaining that *they* are all married!"

It was a festive party with throngs of people in a beautiful setting. After a while I didn't want to be there—so I left and went to my neighborhood cafe to hear my favorite piano player, totally content to be alone enjoying the music.

I asked myself why I didn't want to be at the party. Everyone seemed to be having such a good time. What was the difference between them and me? Then it came to me. They all were there wanting to meet someone—and I didn't. I realized I'm not ready just yet. I like the deliciousness of being unattached. Dates are even an intrusion lately. There are so many things I want to do for me.

No, I'm not ready to meet someone just yet.

I love feeling whole. I wish I had learned the lesson sooner . . . or perhaps it was *too* soon then and the message would have found deaf ears.

I've learned to like who I am. If I had a friend like me, I would say, "Now that is an OK person." There are many people out there who would agree. As far as the others go, I'll just say hello—and quickly say good-bye.

I know this is just the beginning. Nothing can stop me now. I have reached the top of the mountain and I feel as though I can soar. I worked so hard and fought so many battles in making that Journey inward. But, I would have rather died than not made that difficult Journey. It is the only way I know of to find one's Self.

The joy of becoming whole is always accompanied by tears. Every step toward a healthy body, mind, and soul asks that we say good-bye to something familiar. I have never been very good with good-byes. So, as I sit here feeling healthier than I ever felt before, I am also crying.

We think of our lives in terms of permanence, not moments, and we hang on for dear life. If you think about it, isn't all of life about beginnings and endings. The secret is knowing when to let go. When we try to hang on or re-create instead of going on to a next moment, we can only have lesser experiences. We have to close the past to fully enjoy today.

Only for the moment . . . then we must say good-bye.

If we don't make the Journey inward, we will forever be alone. Once we find our Self, we are never alone.

I now know what my next step must be. I've become strong. I've learned how to take care of myself. Now the really difficult part—*to open my Heart*. I know it has risks. When the Heart opens it is so vulnerable. It can get wounded so easily. But I now know I will always recover. I will always reach the other shore.

When the Heart opens up, warm tears of both joy and sadness flow easily. *Joy* from the feeling of oneness with all things that are human. *Sadness* that we reject so much of what is human.

The sweet tears of softness and appreciation that are now starting to flow reassure me that one day I'll be able to let someone in. Strength tempered with softness is magnificent. I feel very good with my strength. I know I will feel magnificent when I allow the nourishing tears of love in again.

My life is beautiful,
I have it all . . .
But even in the sunshine . . .
One has to cry sometimes.

Epilogue

Susan Jeffers finally did allow her Heart to open. And in walked a beautiful Soul named Mark Shelmerdine. Today they are married and together they are discovering what it feels like to truly love and be loved. They practice all the time. And I have it on the best authority that Susan is happier now than she has ever been in her entire life.

About the Author

Susan Jeffers, Ph.D., is a noted public speaker, work-shop leader, and media personality. She has created numerous audio tapes on the subjects of fear, relationships, and personal growth and is the author of *Feel the Fear and Do It Anyway, Opening Our Hearts to Men, Dare to Connect,* and the "Fear-Less" series of affirmation books (*Inner Talk for a Love That Works, Inner Talk for Peace of Mind,* and *Inner Talk for a Confident Day*). Dr. Jeffers lives with her husband in New Mexico.